To Dr. Seuss, who taught me the power of **imagination** and the importance of a **daydream.**
-C.L.

First published by Experience Early Learning Company
7243 Scotchwood Lane, Grawn, Michigan 49637 USA

Text Copyright © 2018 by Experience Early Learning Co.
Manufactured in No.8, Yin Li Street, Tian He District, Guangzhou,
Guangdong, China by Sun Fly Printing Limited
3rd Printing 04/2024

ISBN: 978-1-937954-43-7
Visit us at www.ExperienceEarlyLearning.com

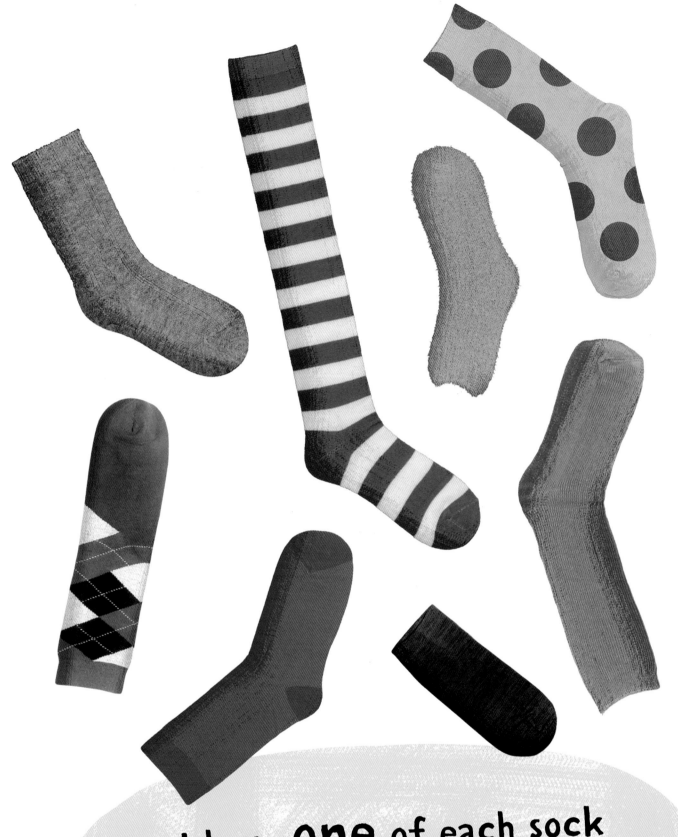

I have **one** of each sock
but the others
have gone **missing.**

HEY!

I have an idea.

If we use our imaginations, we can turn finding my socks into a game.

We can pretend we are searching for wild animals.

Let's go on a...

We can pretend it's a deep, dark cave.

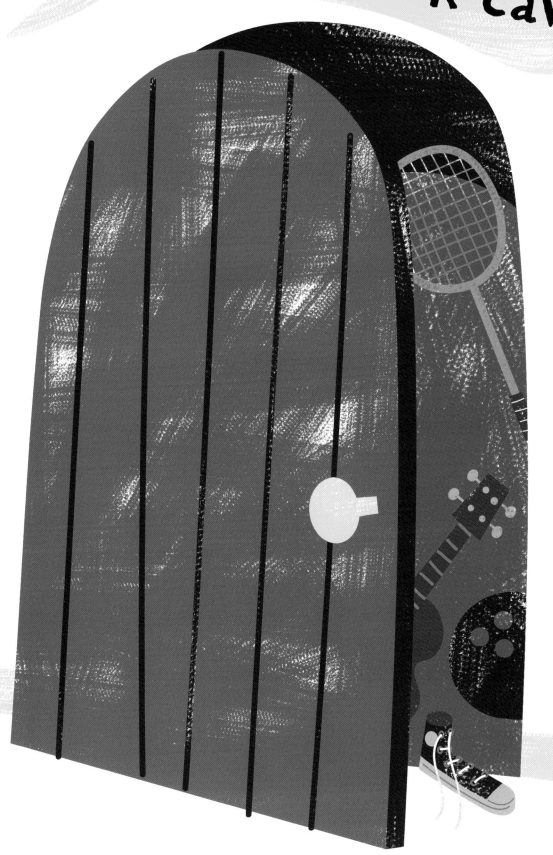

A bat!

How about we look
under my bed?

Imagine it's a **giant** fallen tree.

What might prowl
under a fallen tree?

What might
hang around

or lurk in the water below
a mighty waterfall?

A snake
and
a crocodile!
You found them both!

It will
take us
deeper
into the
jungle.

**Are you
ready?**

An elephant!

What might
splish

and splash
around the
watering hole?

A giraffe

and a flamingo!

We can pretend we are searching high up in the treetops!

What might swing **way up** in the treetops?

A monkey!

WE DID IT!

What an **adventure!**
A little **imagination** can make anything fun!

The End ?